A Prospect of Norwich

Norwich by Rowlandson 1799

By pleasant views and villas bounded,
By shelt'ring hills and woods surrounded:
Above, a wide expanse of fields
A pure and constant fragrance yields;
Below, two silver streamlets meet,
And lay their tribute at its feet

A Norfolk Tale 1792

Prospect Press

A Prospect of Norwich

By George Nobbs

First published August 2003

0-9545521-1-3 H/BK
0-9545521-2-1 P/BK

Acknowledgements

This book owes much to the generosity and patience of Mr Ron Fiske who so kindly allowed the reproduction of many prints in his collection. Mr Raymond Frostick was equally generous in the sphere of maps, and of course, I must thank all the staff of the excellent Heritage Centre at the Millenium Library in Norwich for their help.

Contents

Published by
Prospect Press
Native Guides Ltd

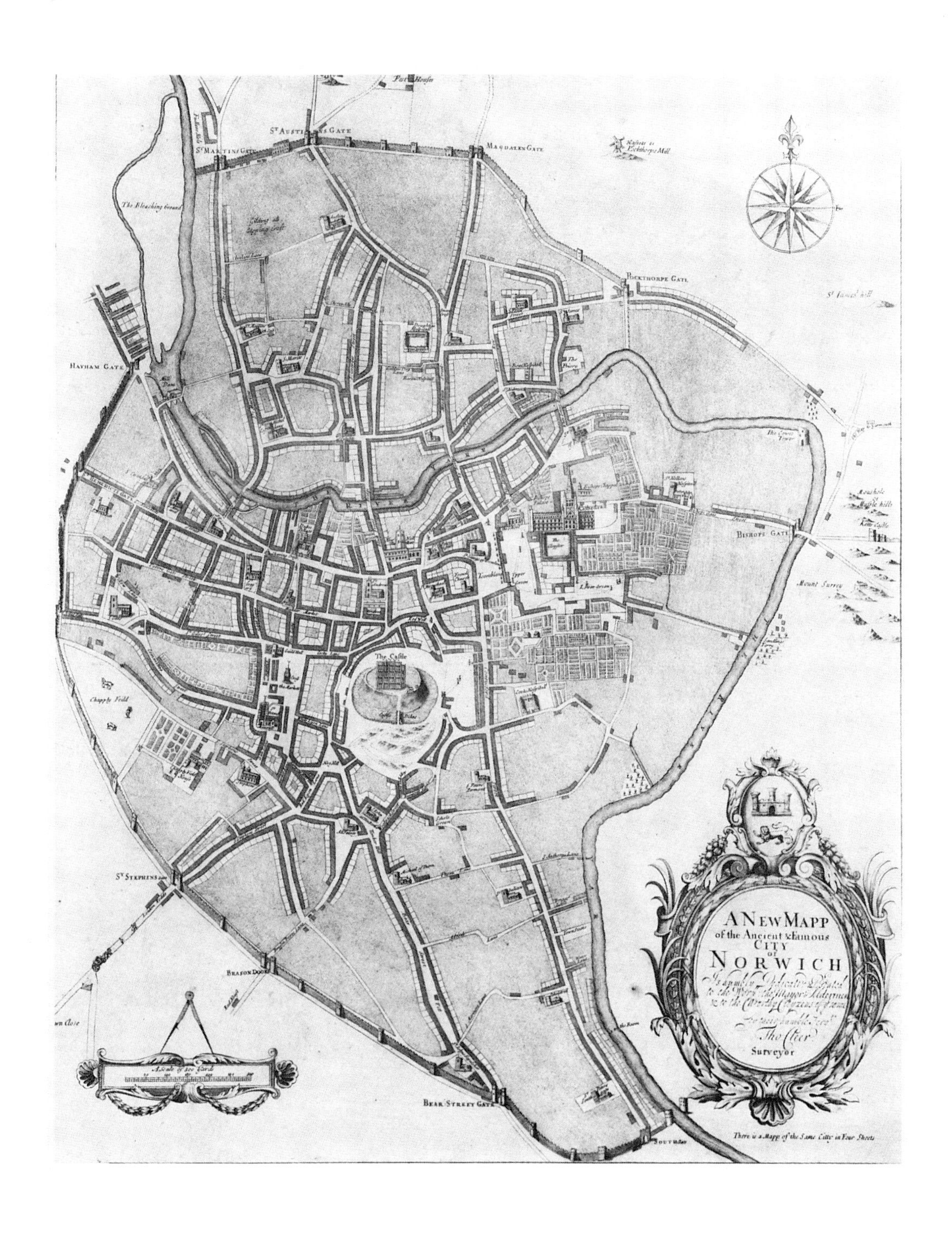

Thomas Cleer's Map of 1698

May God give you the same loving peace and riches as we have here in Norwich *Flemish Refugee writing to his wife. Jan 1564*

There is great trade doing . . . when you come to Norwich you shall find gold. *Letter of two Dutch boys who had fled to Norwich in 1565, writing to their father.*

This City, self-supplied, should England need
a capital,might fairly take the lead. *Arthur Johnson 1600*

Norwich is either a city in an orchard, or an orchard in a city, so equally are the houses and trees blended in it, so that the pleasure of the country and the populousness of the city meet here together. Yet in this mixture, the inhabitants participate nothing of the rusticalness of the one, but altogether of the urbanity and civility of the other. *Thomas Fuller 1662*

The City is pleasantly situated nearly in the centre of the county of Norfolk, in the latitude of 52 deg. 42 min. N. 112 miles North-east from London, in the midst of a fertile country, agreeably interspersed with delightful villas and gentlemen's seats. The roads are spacious and good, most of them being turnpikes, and the magistrates of the present day will be entitled to the thanks of posterity, for their attention to everything which can improve the appearance, and contribute to the general welfare of the city.

The inhabitants in general are remarked for their urbanity, hospitality, and the readiness with which they contribute to all public and private charitable institutions, the better classes for their taste and munificence; and greatly to the credit of the lower classes, much less of that inclination to dissoluteness of manners prevails amongst them than is usually found in large and populous cities. So strict is the attention of the magistrates, in checking in its earliest existance the progress of vice and immorality, that the execution of a criminal in the city does not occur for many years together; there have lately been instances both at at assizes and sessions when not a single prisoner has appeared on the calendar for trial.

The city contains within its liberty one cathedral and thirty-eight parish churches, two foreign churches, two Roman catholic chapels, three presbyterian, one independent, four anabaptist, three methodist, and two quaker's meeting-houses, three public halls, three common prisons, eight public hospitals, eleven charity schools, one dispensary, seven common bridges, a theatre-royal and an assembly-house, horse and foot barracks, 8396 houses, and above 37,000 inhabitants.

For the better preservation of the peace, the city is divided into four great wards, called Conisford ward, Mancroft ward, Wymer ward, and the North ward: these are subdivided into three smaller divisions, each of which is under the jurisdiction of an alderman and two constables. The streets are lighted by lamps in the winter season.There are also firemen, who are always ready in case of an accident happening by fire; and there are several engines in the guildhall and parish churches, with fire buckets and plugs, belonging to the water-works, which likewise supply the inhabitants with water, brought to the houses by pipes laid under the streets, in the same manner as the new river water-works in London.

The greatest extent of the city within the walls, from the north to the south, is about two miles; and from the west to the east, more than a mile. The walls are said to include a space of more than three miles in circumference, but the whole has never been built upon, large portions of ground in the extremities next the walls being laid out in gardens and orchards, which gives the city a more rural appearance than many towns of not one quarter of its extent; beside the large open spaces of chapel-field and the castle-ditches. The hamlets in the liberty without the walls are very thinly inhabited, and extend about a mile from the gates on the east side of the city, and two miles on the sides of the south and west. *The History of Norwich. P. Browne 1814*

Introduction

So many are the fables, and so various the accounts that we have , of the origins of this City, that it be trouble to no purpose, to recount them all; to pass by therefore the stories of King Gurgunt's founding the Castle, and calling it after his own name; or that of Julius Caesar's building the walls thereof, and naming it Blancheflower, from Blanche, his kinswoman, whom he is pretended to have married to King Lud's son, or to follow the tradition of Polidore Virgil and others, recited by Nevil, who pretend to find something of Norwicus in the name of Ordovices, a people of Britain, far enough distant from hence;I shall rather choose to give such an account of it as is most consonant to reason,and agreeable to truth, as far as is evident from such records as we have left to us.

So wrote the Reverend Francis Blomefield in his monumental history of Norfolk. He published his work at intervals from 1739 until his death in 1751 and to a greater or lesser extent all histories of Norwich and Norfolk owe something to his multiple-volumed "Essay towards a Topographical History of the County of Norfolk".

Blomefield was typical of the age in which he lived.Born in the Hall next to the church, he was rector of Fersfield in Norfolk for twenty-three years. During that time he devoted himself almost entirely to researching and compiling his history, setting up his own printing press which was disastrously destroyed by fire along with the first edition of his work. He lived in a house in Willow Lane in Norwich,in an area that was to see considerable rebuilding during the 18th and early 19th centuries. Over a half a century later the young George Borrow was to live in a house practically next-door and he too would see and write about the Norwich that he loved so well.

Exactly one hundred years after Blomefield's death, Borrow published "Lavengro" which contains a description of Norwich which is so frequently quoted (though almost always abridged).

There is a fine old city before us, and first of that let me speak.

A fine old city truly is that, view it from whatever side you will; but it shows best from the east,where the ground, bold and elevated, overlooks the fair and fertile valley in which it stands.Gazing from those heights the eye beholds a scene which cannot fail to awaken, even in the least sensitive bosom, feelings of pleasure and admiration. At the foot of the heights flows a narrow and deep river, with an antique bridge communicating with a long and narrow suburb, flanked on either side by rich meadows of the brightest green, beyond which spreads the city; the fine old city, perhaps the most curious specimen at present extant of the genuine old English town. Yes, there it spreads from north to south, with its venerable houses, its numerous gardens, its thrice twelve churches, its mighty mound, which, if tradition speaks true, was raised by human hands to serve as the grave heap of an old heathen king, who sits deep within it, with his sword in his hand, and his gold and silver treasures about him. There is a grey old castle upon the top of that mighty mound; and yonder,rising three hundred feet above the soil, from among those noble forest trees, behold that old Norman master-work, that cloud-encircled cathedral spire, around which a garrulous army of rooks and choughs continually wheel their flight. Now who can wonder that the children of that fine old city are proud of her and offer up prayers for her prosperity.

Borrow was describing the city that he grew up in when the Norwich School of Artists and the very people who created the illustrations in this book were his contemporaries as were the members of the literary circle who could describe Norwich as the Athens of England and be justified in doing so. These were remarkable times for Norwich; economically, intellectually, and artistically the City had reached its zenith but even as the later engravings were being produced Norwich was beginning to be overtaken by the new industrial cities of the North and the Midlands.

The pictures shown here are chiefly the work of John Sell Cotman, James Stark, James Sillet and John Ninham; they were depicting a City that had, for centuries, been either the second or third city of England and which yielded to none in intellectual, economic, or artistic pre-eminence. It is only with hindsight that we see these prints and engraving as depicting a world that was passing – to the members of the Norwich School of Artists as well as to writers like Borrow Norwich was what it had been for as long as anybody could remember, the most important City outside London. And one with a history to match, as Borrrow related

Ah! there is good blood in that old city, and in the whole circumjacent region of which it is the capital. The Angles possessed the land at an early period, which, however, they were eventually to share with hordes of Danes and Northmen, who flocked thither across the sea to found hearthsteads on its fertile soil. The present race, a mixture of Angles and Danes, still preserve much which speaks strongly of their northern ancestry; amongst them ye will find the light-brown hair of the north, the strong and burly forms of the north, many a wild superstition, ay, and many a wild name connected with the ancient history of the north and its sublme mythology; the warm heart, and the strong heart of the old Danes and Saxons still beat in those regions, and there ye will find, if anywhere, old northern hospitality and kindness of manner,united with energy, perseverance, and dauntless intrepidity; better soldiers or mariners never bled in their country's battles than those nurtured in those regions, and within those old walls. It was yonder, to the west, that the great naval hero of Britain first saw the light; he who annihilated the sea pride of Spain, and dragged the humbled banner of France in triumph at his stern. He was born yonder, towards the west, and of him there is a glorious relic in that old town; in its dark flint guildhouse, the roof of which you can just descry rising above the mass of buildings, in the upper hall of justice, is a species of glass shrine, in which the relic is to be seen; a sword of curious workmanship, the blade is of keen Toledan steel, the heft of ivory and mother-of-pearl.'Tis the sword of Cordova,won in bloodiest fray off Saint Vincent's promontory, and presented by Nelson to the old capital of the much-loved land of his birth. Yes, the proud Spaniard's sword is to be seen in yonder guildhouse in its glass case affixed to the wall: many other relics has the good old town, but none prouder than the Spaniard's sword.

Such was the place to which, when the war was over, my father retired."

It is interesting that Borrow did not mention Kett's Rebellion, or the Civil War, but his sympathies and those of virtually all his circle would have been with Kett in this most radical city. Norwich was known to the government as "the Jacobin City" and they sent spies to report on its citzens and their societies. When staying in Aylsham in 1792, Fanny Burney wrote, "I am truly amazed to find this country filled with little revolution societies which transmit their notions to the larger committee at Norwich which communicates the whole to the reformers in London. I am told there is scarcely a village in Norfolk free from these meetings". Borrow had been born in 1803 the year before republican enthusiasm reached such a peak in Norwich that the landlord of the Kings Arms in Elm Hill found it wise to change its name to the Britons Arms. Borrow chose instead to focus on Nelson – a hero to all shades of Norwich opinion. Nor did he mention along with the Angles and Danes, the Dutch and Flemish who almost doubled the population of Elizabethan Norwich. But he probably felt he had no need to, for they were kinsmen coming, after all, from the same stock.

Just as Francis Blomefield was typical of the painstaking 18th century antiquarian, concerned with refuting the wildly fanciful stories of Norwich's origins, so Borrow personified the early 19th century romantic with his story of an ancient heathen king, sword in hand, surrounded by his treasure. But nonetheless, Borrow certainly painted an accurate picture of Norwich's own estimation of itself on the eve of the Railway Age.

Such then was the Norwich depicted in these engravings and lithographs; on the pages which follow we will, where possible, allow the writings of the period to speak for themselves.

The Castle

. . . a terrace falls
With gentle slopes from those dread walls
Where beauty holds its daily court
And all the Norwich belles resort
A Norfolk Tale 1792

Vulgar chronology will have Norwich Castle as old as Julius Caesar; but his distance from these parts, and the gothick form of structure, abridgeth such antiquary Sir Thomas Browne 1658

I have already had occasion to mention this castle. It is the remains of what was once a Norman stronghold, and is perched upon a round mound or monticle, in the midst of the old city. Steep is the mound and scarped, evidently by the hand of man; a deep gorge, over which is flung a bridge, seperates it, on the south, from a broad swell of open ground called "the hill"; of old the scene of many a tournament and feat of Norman chivalry, but now much used as a show-place for cattle, where those who buy and sell beeves and other beasts resort at stated periods George Borrow , Lavengro 1851

Despite the prevailing 18th century belief that it was built in 575, Norwich Castle and its mound was the work of the Normans. William the Conqueror first granted the castle to Earl Ralph Guader but after his rebellion of 1075, gave it to Roger Bigod during whose time the present keep was built. He too rebelled in 1087 but managed to retain his office as did his family who continued to be Earls, constables of the Castle and governors of the City despite more rebellions until the 13th century.

Its greatest moment of excitement, apart from the frequent Bigod rebellions, was its capture by French troops and assorted English traitors, under the command of Lewis the Dauphin in 1216. They were taking advantage of the death of King John and the youth of his son the 9 year-old Henry III and stayed holed up in the castle for several months before withdrawing. In 1340 it became the gaol for the county of Norfolk which it remained until the 1890s when it was converted into a museum.

Norwich Castle (opposite)
The print dates from 1738 and shows the then dilapidated state of the structure.

Norwich Castle (below)
In 1312 Thomas de Brotherton, the new constable of the castle "repaired and beautified the building and crowned the upper part with new battlements". These were again replaced at the beginning of the 18th century and then, between 1790 and 1793, the interior underwent an "entire alteration" and outside, next the keep, "a vast pile of building was completed, somewhat resembling the architecture of the old castle, to the east of which it adjoins, and called the New County Gaol. The walls are built of Scotch Granite and are very strong, massive, and solid. The outside has a very heavy and inelegant appearance". So said Browne's History in 1814, one year after this print appeared in Britton's *Architectural Antiquities of Great Britain*. The design of this shortlived structure was by Sir John Soane.

In 1774 the sides of the mound were planted with trees "at considerable expence to the county, although it answered very little purpose at the time; but soon afterwards the ditch was divided into various allotments, which were given to such persons as chose to accept them, on condition of keeping up the fences. By this means the hill has been kept in good repair, the plantations on the sides are in a flourishing state, and the gardens in the bottom, differing in style from each other, according to the respective tastes of the several occupiers, produce so pleasing an effect, that strangers have acknowledged the general view of the gardens and of the city, from the summit of the hill, to be one of the most agreeable prospects in Europe."

Norwich Castle (above)
This 1834 view, from roughly the same viewpoint as the previous print, shows the present range of buildings which replaced Sir John Soane's design. It also shows the improvements which were made to the gardens when the castle was transferred from the Crown to the county of Norfolk in 1805. "An elegant iron railing, elevated on a stone base of peculiar neat and excellent workmanship, has since been erected, inclosing the edge of the hill, the extremity of the ditch, and the parapet of the bridge. The admissions to the gardens at the foot of the hill is by six iron gates, between columns of free stone, and the whole lighted by lamps. At the foot of the bridge are erected two square towers of Portland stone, forming a complete porter's lodge, with gates of cast iron, of which there is another at the back descent of the hill: these gates are kept closed at night, and secure the premises from the intrusions of ill-disposed persons, and tend to prevent the escape of any of the prisoners, or the commission of any depredations on the property of the occupiers of the gardens."

Norwich Castle (below)
This 1842 print also shows the new prison buildings which William Wilkins designed in 1825. (It was his father who had re-modelled the interior of the Keep in 1793). This new prison was to house 224 male prisoners and all the requirements of a gaol for not more than £26,000. It now forms the basis of the museum's galleries housing, among much else, the remarkable Colman Bequest of Norwich School paintings.

In 1795 William Wilkins senior had published an essay "proving" that King Uffa had built his castle in 575 and that the inhabitants of Venta Icenorum came to Norwich and sheltered around it for safety. In 642 it was, he wrote, a royal castle of King Anna and was later held by King Edmund, the Danes, Alfred, Swein, Ulfkettle, and Canute. All this was fanciful nonsense but it was widely believed.

The print also shows the result of Salvin's restoration, carried out between 1834 and 1839. The artists of the Norwich School for the most part deplored it and this print was not produced by one of their number. Salvin, although using Bath stone, in place of Caen, to reface the crumbling façade remained faithful to the original design and decoration and undoubtedly saved the castle from a worse fate. He did similar work for both Windsor and the Tower of London.

The presence of farm animals reminds us that the site now forming Castle Mall Park was a cattle-market from the time of James II until 1960. Public hangings used to take place between the two gatehouses at the foot of the bridge and Charles Dickens, passing through in 1849, found Norwich "a disappointment, all save its place of execution, which we found fit for a gigantic scoundrels exit".

The River Wensum

Here too each city youth and sprightly lass,
In the gay sailing boats are seen to pass,
Adown sweet Wensum's stream on pleasure's wing,
Making with with joy the fruitful vale to ring
James Lamb 1820

The City of Norwich is said to occupy a larger space of ground, comparative with its population, than any other in the kingdom. The river Wensum approaches the town on the north-west, and leaves it to the south-east; but between these extreme points, it pursues so bold and beautiful a serpentine course, as to trace for a brief way the western limit – describe a semicircle round one-fourth of the town, on its left or north bank – sweep sinuously past a thinly edificed area – and finally move along the eastern skirts of the compact field of houses. A gentle acclivity extends along the right bank of the river, and terminates near its last bend; and this height bears on its summit and its slopes, all the more ancient parts of the city, and a large proportion of its present streets and buildings.

The shape or plan of the town as marked by its ancient boundaries, approaches that of a cornucopia, or bent cone, extending more than a mile and a half in length from north to south, on both sides of the river, and one mile and a quarter in its greatest breadth; but these measurements are consideably extended by modern erections, especially on the west and south-west. Francis White: History, Gazetteer and Directory of Norfolk and the City and County of Norwich 1854

The River Wensum, and the course it takes at this point, is the reason for Norwich's existence. The City grew around the point where the river was fordable near the crossing of two Roman tracks. Conesford, now Kings Street and Tombland, became the centre of the Anglian town, to which were added Danish and Norman centres. The people of Norwich named this river, from its source to the sea, Wensum; the people of Yarmouth, some time later, naming it from the sea, called it Yare. Wensum is, of course, the proper name for the whole river.

The Valley of Thorpe from Butter Hills (opposite above)
This charming 1842 lithograph by Miles Cotman, son of the great John, shows the river valley at Thorpe from Richmond Hills, at the top of Bracondale. These had been a Pleasure Garden on the inside of the City Walls. The Area was also known as Butter Hills from the Butter Tower, itself a corruption of Butler from John Le Boteler who gave the hills to Carrow Abbey. Hidden from view, on the right, is Carrow Hill, built to give work to ex-soldiers after the Napoleonic War.

Hinsby's Gardens, Thorpe (opposite below)
From Richmond Hills you could see this area, called "The Richmond of Norfolk". It is still a popular spot for the citizens of Norwich whose boundary extends along the river, and its banks, all the way to Hardley Cross near Loddon.

The View near Carrow Bridge (below)
This picture, like the previous one and the next two, was drawn by James Stark as part of a collection which he published in 1833 to celebrate "Norwich A Port" one of the great schemes of the 1820s to bypass the port of Yarmouth via the "New Cut" to Lowestoft. Stark explained that the picture of Carrow Bridge was wrong it "having been recently converted into a draw-bridge, for the admission of sea-borne vessels that arrived by the new navigation. The work being sufficiently advanced, the first ship, frieghted with merchandise from London passed through it on 30th of September 1833. On that day Norwich resumed the priviledge of a port which she anciently possessed, and of which she was deprived in these ignorant times, when exclusive jurisdictions of feudal tyranny and chartered monopoly were allowed to bar the free exercise of natural rights and advantages. Thousands of her citizens assembled to hail an event pregnant with such important consequences".

Carrow Bridge had ben built in April 1810 (in August of that year Foundry Bridge was begun) and in 1817 Carrow Hill was constructed giving a route from Ber Street Gates to the Yarmouth road. As for "Norwich A Port", as soon as the New Cut was opened, Yarmouth reduced her harbour dues to below those of Lowestoft, thus rendering the whole scheme redundant.

The Devils Tower or The Boom Towers (opposite above)
These towers, either side of the River, were part of the City Defences and an iron chain, or boom, could be stretched across to stop ships. The present Carrow Bridge stands just the other side of the tower.

Bishops Bridge (opposite below)
This ancient Bridge, built by the Bishops of Norwich, became part of the City Defences in 1393. Its Gate was taken down in 1793.

The Cathedral

The diocese of Norwich is one of the very oldest in England; and for the most part consisted anciently as it still does, of the counties of Norfolk and Suffolk. The See however has not always been where it is now at Norwich. It was first placed at Dunwich, in Suffolk then both at Dunwich and Elmham, in Norfolk, at the same time, the diocese being divided in two parts; then at Elmham only, next, though only for a short time, at Thetford, and lastly at Norwich, the most convenient situation for it, and where therefore we hope it may continue to the end of time. Winkles Cathedrals 1838.

The Cathedral of this city is a fine fabric, and the spire steeple very high and beautiful. It is not ancient, the bishop's see having been first at Thetford; from whence it was not translated hither till the twelth century; yet the church has many antiquities in it. Daniel Defoe 1722

Suffolk obtained its own Cathedral, at Bury St Edmunds, in 1914, but the rest of what *Winkles Cathedrals* has to say is still true; Defoe on the other hand, was wrong about the date of the transfer from Thetford. The facts are as follows: the building's founder Herbert de Losinga was brought up in the monastery of Fescamp in Normandy where he eventually became prior and then chaplain to William Rufus with whom he came to England in 1088. Rufus, upon becoming William II, made him Abbot of Ramsey in Huntingdonshire and Lord Chancellor of England.Becoming rich, Herbert bought the abbotcy of Winchester for his father and the Bishopric of Thetford for himself for £2,900. This was a huge sum in the eleventh century and we are told that "his conscience sharply reproached him for such practices, and repenting of the simony he had been guilty of, he went privately to Rome, and presented himself to Pope Pascal II resigned his pastoral staff into his hands." The Pope granted him absolution on condition of his building and endowing certain churches and monasteries as a penance, and granted him a licence to translate the espiscopical see from Thetford to Norwich .

He laid the foundation stone in 1096 and died on 22 of July 1119 after a full political and espiscopal career and is buried in the centre of the choir.

Thus the Cathedral at Norwich came about; it possesses the second longest nave, second highest spire, and largest monastic cloisters in England. Apart from the wholly justified riot of 1272, "news of which shocked Christendom", and the spire falling down both in 1361 and 1463, its history has been mostly uneventful. Indeed by the early 19th century under the mostly absentee Bishop Bathurst who presided for thirty-two years till death removed him at the age of 93, Norwich had become such a byword for every kind of clerical laxness that it was known as "The Dead See". His successor in 1837,

Cathedral from Butter Hills (opposite above)
The West Front of the Cathedral (above)

Bishop Stanley, shunned by many on account of his zeal to reform abuses, his support of liberal causes, and his friendship with the world-famous singer Jenny Lind, had, by the time of his death in 1849, so overcome local predudice and restored the reputation of the dioscese, that it was said of his funeral "Nothing like it had been seen in Norwich Cathedral since the Reformation – And I very much doubt in any other Cathedral in England".

Henry Bathurst , "this amiable and venerable prelate" as Winkle decribed him, although a friend of nonconformists and a supporter of both Catholic Emancipation and Parliamentary Reform (indeed he was alone amongst the bishops in voting for it) was in all other respects a typical 18th century cleric. The brother of Pitt's friend the Earl of Bathurst, he was for many years an absentee Norfolk rector and Parson Woodforde collected his tithes for him. Woodforde served under four Bishops of Norwich but did not live to see his old friend enthroned in Norwich Cathedral; he did however leave an account of the early weeks of his second Bishop, Dr Bagot, who appears to to have been something of a new broom – "a prelate of extra-ordinary abilities, of fervent piety, and most exemplary life ..reforming abuses and insisting on a strict attention of the clergy to their pastoral duties" said Browne's History.

"Oct 12 1783 Had another disagreeable Letter this morning from the Bishop's Register to preach at the Cathedral of Norwich on the Sunday Morn' Feb:8 next.

"Oct 24 1783 After breakfast I dressed myself in my best Coat and Waistcoat and then walked down in my Boots to the Bishops Palace and had a long conversation with the Bishop about many things – but what I went to see his Lordship chiefly on, was my being appointed on the Combination List to preach at the Cathedral on the 8th. of Febuary next, when my name had been inserted but a few years back. To which his Lordship replied, that as I did not then preach in Person was one reason, and the second was that he was willing that the Pulpit at the Cathedral should be filled properly by able and beneficed Clergy and that it was rather a Compliment conferred by him on those that he so appointed.

" Febuary Feb. 8 1784. At 10.O'clock this morning we all went in a coach to the Cathedral. I went fully dressed and being Preacher sat next the Sub-Dean Dr Hammond. Whilst the Anthem was singing I was conducted by the Virger to the Pulpit and there preached a sermon on these words 'Let your light so shine before Men that they see your good works and glorify your Father wch. Is in Heaven'. Neither Bishop, Dean or Mayor at the Cathedral.The Cathedral was not crowded owing to the cold."

Woodforde died during the shortlived " Peace of Amiens" which was formally proclaimed on Tuesday 4th of May 1802. That night's festivities included an early example of floodlighting the Cathedral as the *Norwich Mercury* reported:

"The most striking and awful effect of the illuminations arose to the mind on the contemplation of the churches whose towers and walls wore an air of solemn stillness and grandeur which it is almost impossible to describe. The spire of the cathedral was particularly sublime from the reflection of the lights on one side and the deep unchanging darkness on the other."

The Erpingham Gate (opposite)
The previous picture comes from the book on Norwich Cathedral published in 1816 by John Britton who was an honorary member of the Norwich Society of Artists and a friend of John Sell Cotman who published this view in 1818. Sir Thomas Erpingham, whose house stood nearby, was commander of the English archers at the battle of Agincourt and a bosom friend of Henry V but this did not prevent him from being pursued by the Prior of the Cathedral monastery who accused him of "supporting the doctrines of Wycliffe" and forced him to pay for the building of this gate as a penance.

The Ethelbert Gate (above)
Two views of another forced penance. In 1272 the Cathedral monks, supported by mercenary troops from Yarmouth, attacked the citizens of Norwich. So great was the riot that ensued that the King summoned a special parliament at Bury St Edmunds "to advise him how to proceed against the citizens for these heinous transgressions". For the offence of defending themselves, 34 citizens were executed by being drawn by horses, others were hung drawn and quartered, while many women were burnt to death, massive fines were imposed on the city and individuals, our liberties were forfeited and the citizens were required to build new gates. The one seen here also replaced the old chapel of St Ethelbert which had been destroyed in the riot. The Prior of Norwich, who was generally recognised as the instigator of the whole affair, was required to resign.

At the time that these prints were published in 1815 the top of the Gate had just been restored by William Wilkins. The exterior is on the left, interior on the right.

The Alnwick Gate (above)
Cotman's etching of 1814 shows the Gate to the bishop's palace built by William Alnwick, Keeper of the Privy Seal for Henry V, and Bishop from 1425 to 1436. Apart from fierce fighting all around it during Kett's Rebellion, its life has been uneventful. Nine years after etching this Gate Cotman came to live in the house opposite, which still stands.

The Nave (opposite)
This 1816 print from Britton's History, shows one of Norwich Cathedral's chief glories. "Sometimes it has been crowded with altars, adorned with shrines, enriched with offerings, and honoured with the presence of many English sovereigns, attended by their courtiers, the prelacy, the body of the clergy, and the corporation of the magistracy: at other times it has been defaced, plundered, and profaned in the civil commotions. From the year1740 it has been in the state of progressive improvement, the inside having been thoroughly repaired and completely adorned and beautified". Browne 1814.

Pulls Ferry (above)
This was the ancient watergate to the cathedral as it looked in 1834 – and still does. From here was unloaded the Caen stone, trans-shipped from Yarmouth, that was used to build the cathedral. Until about 1780, the original canal through the Close still existed but was then filled in.The picturesque house on the left of the arch was an inn kept, in the early 19th century, by the ferryman Mr Pull. Before his time it had been known as Sandling's Ferry after a ferryman who had been a cathedral chorister in the reign of the great Elizabeth.

Corbridge's Plan (overleaf)
This map or plan published in 1727 shows all the medieval churches within the City Walls together with the houses of 15 leading citizens. Whilst the churches can still be identified, only one of the houses (in Princes Street) can.

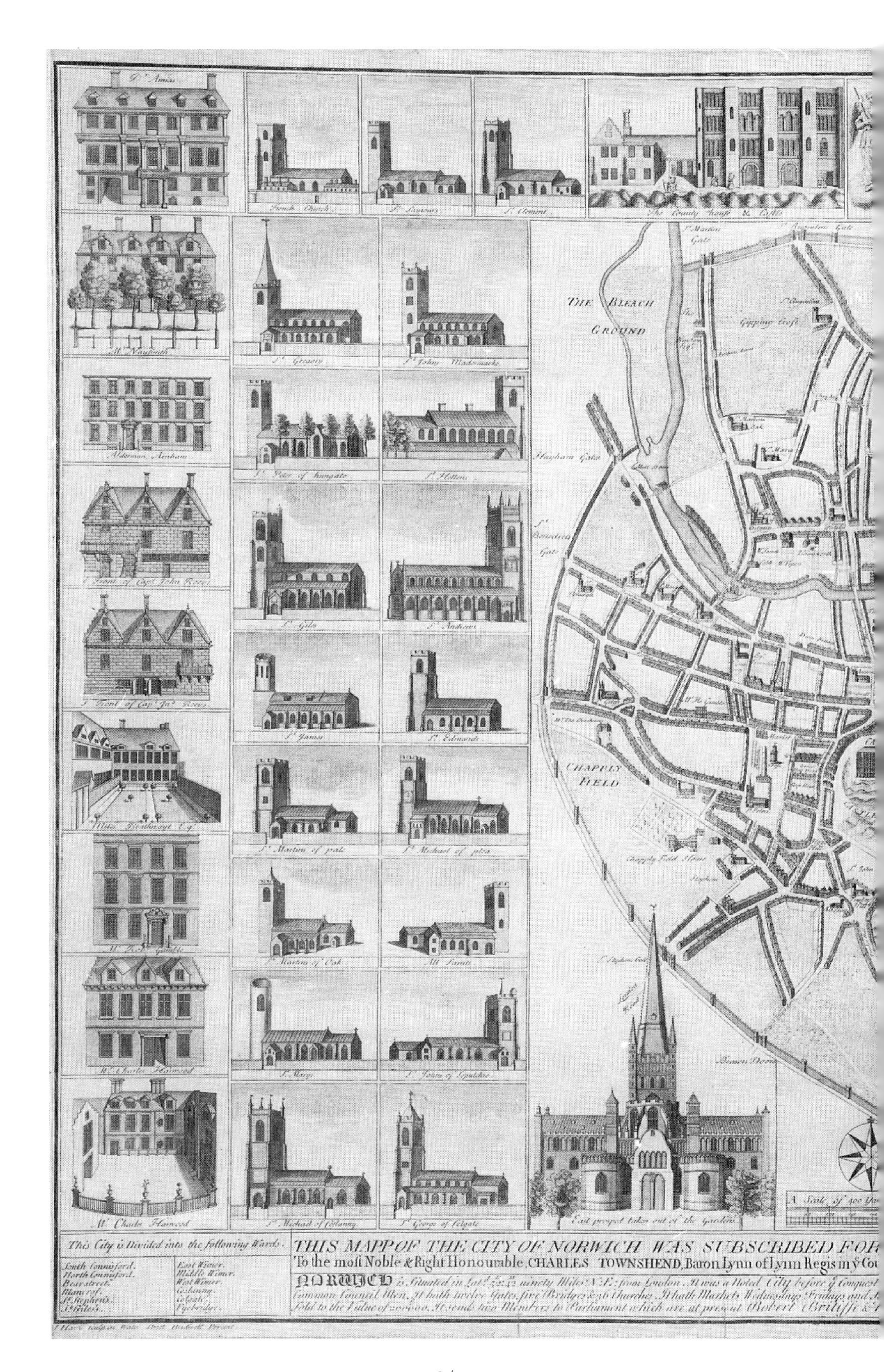

Dr. Amias
French Church
St. Simons
St. Clemint
The County house & Castle
Mr. Naysmith
St. Gregory
St. John Madermarket
Alderman Ankam
St. Peter of hungate
St. Hellens
St. Giles
St. Andrews
St. James
St. Edmonds
St. Martin of pale
St. Michael of plea
St. Martin of Oak
All Saints
St. Marys
St. John of Sepulchre
Mr. Charles Harwood
St. Michael of Cosslanny
St. George of Colgate
East prospect taken out of the Garden
THE BLEACH GROUND
CHAPPLY FIELD
Heyham Gate
St. Martins Gate
St. Augustins Gate
Gipping Croft
Chapply Field House
A Scale of 400 Yards
This City is Divided into the following Wards.
South Connisford.
North Connisford.
Bearstreet.
Mancrof.
St. Stephens.
St. Giles.
East Wimer.
Middle Wimer.
West Wimer.
Coslanny.
Colgate.
Fyebridge.
THIS MAPP OF THE CITY OF NORWICH WAS SUBSCRIBED FOR
To the most Noble & Right Honourable, CHARLES TOWNSHEND, Baron Lynn of Lynn Regis in ye Cou
NORWICH is Situated in Latd. 52:42 ninety Miles N.E. from London. It was a Noted City before ye Conquest
Common Councel Men. It hath twelve Gates, five Bridges & 36 Churches. It hath Markets Wednesdays Fridays and
sold to the Value of 200000. It sends two Members to Parliament which are at present Robert Britiffe &

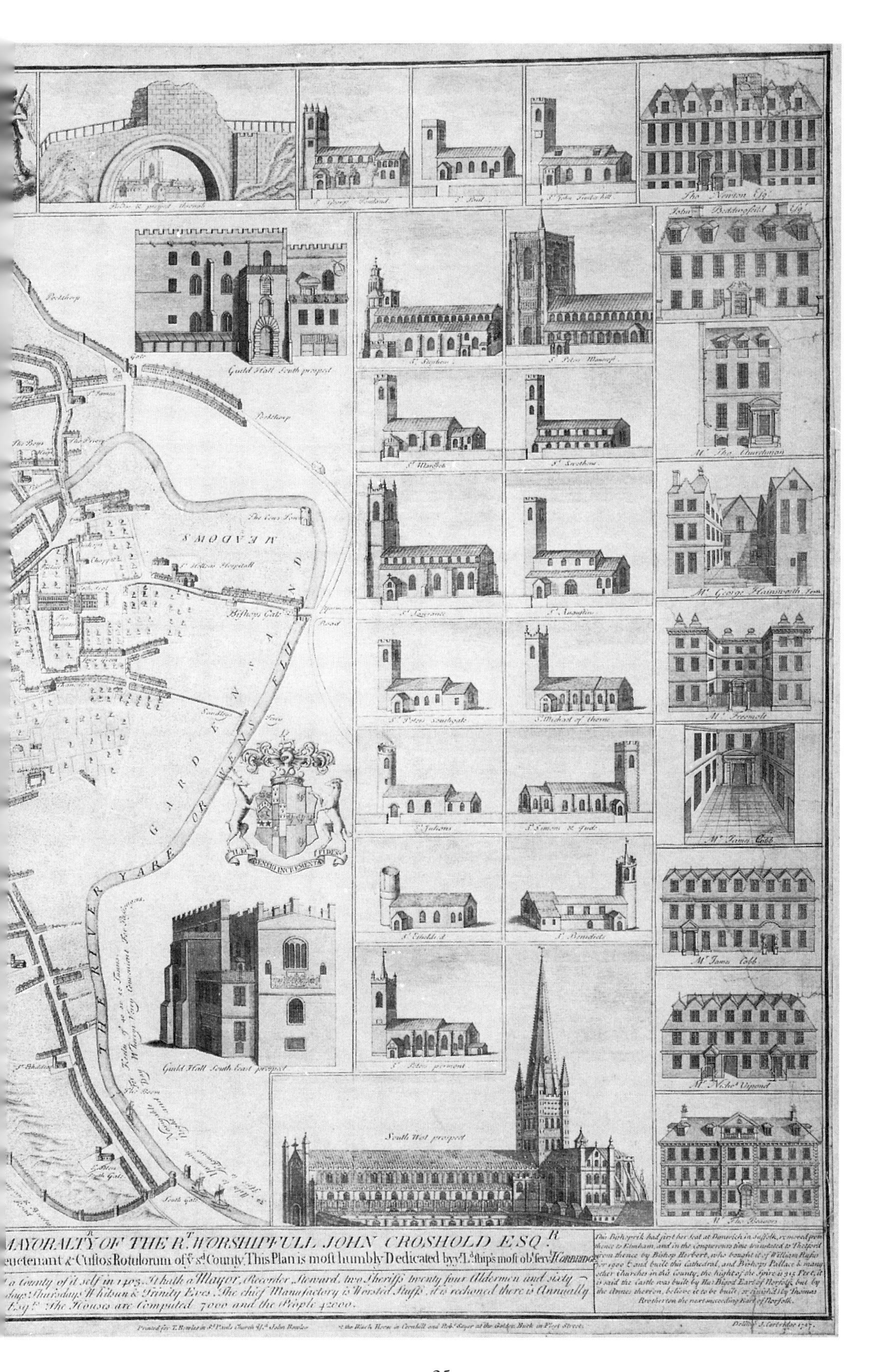
Guild Hall South prospect
St Stephens
St Peter Mancroft
St Lawrence
St Augustin
St Julians
St Simons & Jude
St Benedicts
Guild Hall South East prospect
South West prospect
MEADOWS
Bishops Gate
THE RIVER YARE OR WENSUM
Mr George Hanworth
Mr James Cobb
Mr Nichs Upjohn
MAYORALTY OF THE Rt WORSHIPFULL JOHN CROSHOLD ESQr
euctenant & Custos Rotulorum of ye sd County. This Plan is most humbly Dedicated by yr Ldships most obt servt
a County of it self in 1403. It hath a Mayor, Recorder, Steward, two Sheriffs twenty four Aldermen and sixty
days; Thursdays Whitsun & Trinity Eves. The chief Manufactory is Worsted Stuffs, it is reckoned there is Annually
Esqr. The Houses are Computed 7000 and the People 42000.
This Bishoprik had first her seat at Dunwich in Suffolk, removed from thence to Elmham, and in the Conquerours time translated to Thetford from thence by Bishop Herbert, who bought it of William Rufus for 1900 £ and built this Cathedral, and Bishops Pallace & many other Churches in this County, the hight of the Spire is 315 Feet, it is said the Castle was built by Hu: Bigod Earl of Norfolk, but by the Armes thereon, believe it to be built, or finish'd by Thomas Brotherton the next succeeding Earl of Norfolk.

The East end of Norwich Cathedral (above)
This view, from the eastern end, is the most popular and frequent way of depicting the Cathdral. The view is largely unchanged except that the Lady chapel which was demolished at the beginning of the 16th century has since been replaced by the Royal Norfolk Regiment chapel which was built after the 1914-18 War. Its position is shown by the two filled-in arches in the centre. Its site had been appropriated by the Dean and Chapter for in 1816 Britton says " in this view the artist has omitted a wall and some shrubbery belonging to a gentleman's garden".

Some Churches and Chapels

One thing I observ'd of remarkable in this Citty, that most of the Churchyards (though some of them large enough) were filled up with earth, or rather the congestion of dead bodys one upon another, for want of Earth etc to the top of the Walls, and many above the walls, so as the Churches seem'd to be built in pitts
John Evelyn 1671

Th*ere are in this city thirty-two parishes beside the cathedral, and a great many meeting houses of Dissenters of all denominations*
Daniel Defoe 1722

Th*ere are twelve gates in all and 36 Churches which is to be seen on a clear day altogether, on the Castle walls I told 30 myself; there they are built all of flint well headed or cut which makes them look blackish and shining . . . A great many Descenters are in this Citty.*
Celia Fiennes 1698

The number of Norwich's pre-Reformation churches is legendary; more than the combined total of the next three places, London, Bristol, and York put together. It also has a long and noble history of religious dissent dating back to the time of Wycliffe and the Lollards. As George Borrow wrote of the site outside Bishops Bridge "many a grisly procession has advanced along that suburb, across the old bridge, towards Lollards Hole; furious priests in front, a calm pale martyr in the midst, a pitying multitude behind. It has its martyrs, the venerable old town!" In the reign of Elizabeth 30 Dutch or Flemish families were invited to Norwich to escape the horrors of The Spanish Fury.That was in 1565; by 1569 they numbered 3000 and ten years later 6000. They introduced "The New Draperies" which took Norwich, within a few years, from a stagnant declining town to the second most populous and wealthy city in England. They also re-inforced the City's taste for religious freedom which supported a wave of chapel-building in the next few centuries.

The following prints can only depict the major denominations of the period. It was not, for example, until 1838 that the 29 members of the Jewish congregation began to plan their first synagogue since the 13th century. It was eventually opened in 1849, a year after the Latter Day Saints had built their chapel in St Pauls Opening.

St Andrews Church (previous page)
After St Peter Mancroft, this was the largest parish church in the city and the most protestant amongst the Anglican fold. It was also the last of the pre-Reformation churches to be built, replacing an earlier structure and being completed in 1506. The ancestors of Nelson's mother are buried here.

St Helens Church (above)
With the exception of St Michael at Coslany, all the churches and chapels shown here are taken from lithographs by James Sillett. This church is remarkable for being, for the most part, a medieval hospital or almshouse. Only the central third of the building actually performs the function of a parish church.

St Peter Hungate (opposite above)
The area gained its name (houndgate) because, it is said, the Bishop kept his dogs hereabouts in olden times. The church was one of the first in the city to become redundant and was converted into a delightful museum of church art in the 1930s. Today it is sadly closed. The church itself was was rebuilt by John and Margaret Paston who had a townhouse nearby. It was from this church that the Rev William Bridge was ejected by the persecuting Bishop Wren in 1636.

St John Maddermarket (opposite below)
Madder was a dye for cloth sold next to the church. This church was for many years almost the estate chapel for the Dukes of Nofolk whose palace stood between it and the river. Inside the church is a memorial to Margaret, Duchess of that most stupid and treacherous Duke who later planned to marry Mary Queen of Scots. Margaret was the second of his three wives and died in 1564 aged 23. Her funeral was a sumptuous affair and she is buried in this church although her tomb is at Framlingham.

St Giles (opposite above)
Although the chancel was demolished in 1581, a new one was built in 1866. The Tower, 120 feet high, once had a fire basket which was anciently used as a beacon for shipping in the Wensum below. Curiously it had a curfew or evening bell, founded by John Colton in 1497. "It is rung the summer half year at nine o'clock, and in the winter at eight; the morning bell is tolled at five o'clock in the summer and six in the winter, at the expense of the parish". He had left money for this bell in gratitude for the occasion when he had almost drowned in marshes by the river but had been guided to safety by the bells of St Giles. The curfew bell was last tolled in 1960, the practice having now lapsed.

St Stephens (opposite below)
This view, from the south-west, is an unusual one, for this prettiest of city churches is more often seen from the street. Said to be the site of a chapel of the Castle, the present church is believed to date from 1350 although there have been numerous excellent additions and alterations. Sadly the large date 1601 displayed in the flint-work of the porch, and which I remember as a boy, has been removed.

St Peter Mancroft (below)
This is the principal church of the City used for many civic events as is perhaps befitting something originally built to serve the new Norman township beneath the Castle. The present church was totally rebuilt between 1430 and 1435 although its massive tower was restored, and greatly added to, between 1881 and 1895. When John Wesley was staying in the City in 1757, he wrote, "I scarcely remember ever to have seen a more beautiful parish church; the more so because its beauty results not from foreign ornaments, but from the very fine form and structure of it".

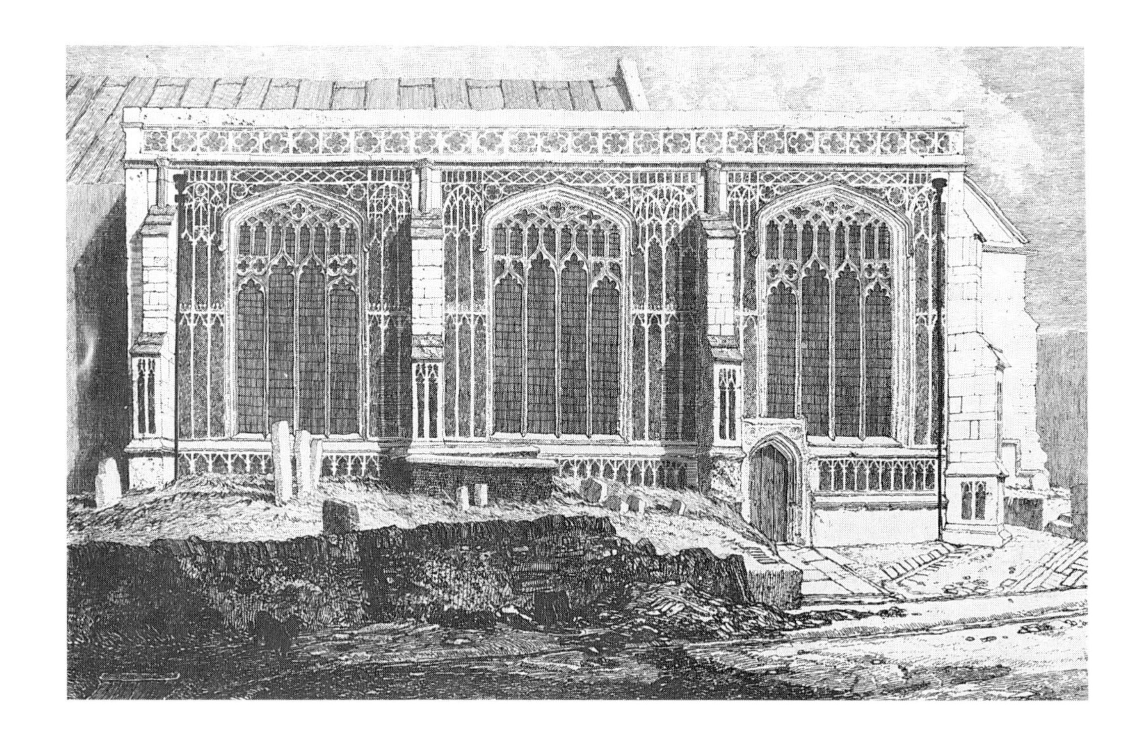

St Michael at Coslany (above)
This is the only Norwich Church that Cotman chose to etch for his monumental 1818 work on Norfolk.It shows the Thorpe chapel built in about 1500 by Robert Thorpe, who had been a member of Parliament for Norwich in the reign of Richard III. It is a magnificent piece of flint flush-work, and Cotman said "this is, I believe, as fine a specimen as Norfolk, or any other county in England, can boast". Cotman also tells us that the chapel was endowed with lands and houses in Norwich and some adjoining villages by Robert Thorpe " who with his three wives, lies buried here; but the inscription over his grave is gone".

The Old Meeting House (opposite)
By the time Mathew Wren became Bishop of Norwich in 1635 he was already chaplain and clerk of the closet to Charles I, Dean of Windsor and an enthusiastic and relentless persecutor. He was described as being very active in "detecting impostures, restraining the reckless and seditious, and breaking the will of all refractory schismatics". One of those whose will he tried to break was the Rev. William Bridges who he ejected from his living at St Peter Hungate church in 1636. Bridges and many of his congregation were forced to flee to Holland where they set up a free church. In 1642 they returned, founding a church in Yarmouth and another in Norwich. Wren (father of the architect) later spent some time in prison.

Evicted at the Restoration, the Norwich followers of Rev. Bridges ended up in Colegate on the site of the old garden of the Blackfriars (whose church had been built by the suspected Lollard Thomas Erpingham) and there they built, in 1693, a Meeting House, "a large and noble building of red brick, very handsomely fronted with four pilasters of the Corinthian order, and has a hipped roof, flat on top. The inside is neatly pewed, with galleries on the east, south and west sides and the pulpit on the north". It is greatly to the credit of the City, that the council, some years ago, made itself responsible for the upkeep of this building which played such a part in the history of what became the Congregational Church.

S. E. VIEW of the OLD INDEPENDENT MEETING HOUSE.

The Octagon Chapel (overleaf)
Almost next door to The Old Meeting House stands The Octagon.The Presbyterians built their meeting house here in 1687 on another part of the former Blackfriars convent, but in 1756 they replaced it by a new chapel designed by Thomas Ivory, Georgian Norwich's favourite architect. "One of the most spacious, noble, and elegant buildings of the kind in the kingdom; justly admired for the neatness and regularity of its structure, as well as for its internal decorations" observed Brown in his History in 1814. Its critics called it "The Devils Cucumber Frame".

John Wesley wrote in November 1757 "I was shown Dr Taylor's new meeting house, perhaps the most elegant one in Europe. It is eight-square, built of the finest brick, with sixteen sash-windows below, and as many above, and eight skylights in the dome, which, indeed, are purely ornamental. The inside is furnished in the highest taste, and is as clean as any nobleman's saloon. The communion table is fine mahogany, the very latches of the pew-doors are polished brass. How can it be thought that the old, coarse gospel should find admission here?"

Although nominally Presbytarian, the Octagon Chapel had by this time become Unitarian and perhaps it was this fact, rather than the elegance of the building that Wesley was referring to in his comments about the old coarse gospel.

Years later, Harriet Martineau recalled her childhood "misery at Chapel". "The Octagon Chapel at Norwich had curious windows in the roof; – not skylights, but letting in light indirectly. I used to sit staring up at those windows and looking for angels to come and take me to heaven, in sight of all the congregation – the end of the world being sure to happen while we were at Chapel".

The Friends Meeting House (opposite above)
The Quakers in Norwich were led by the Gurney family and when in 1797 Prince William Frederick came to Norwich to take command of the army in these parts, he paid court to John Gurney (the Quaker Pope) and the Gurney girls at Earlham on many occasions. They were, at the turning of the 18th and 19th century, a gifted and generous family of whom Elizabeth Fry was the most famous. Not surprisingly therefore the Quakers of Norwich were more accepted than in many other towns and had two chapels and a burial ground. In 1826 they built this chapel in Upper Goat Lane to replace an earlier one. Its architect John Patience also built the Catholic chapel in Willow Lane and the Norfolk and Norwich Subscription Library in Guildhall Hill. When the American Quaker preacher William Savery visited their old meeting house in 1798, the *Norfolk Chronicle* reported that he attracted an audience of nearly 2000!

St Marys Baptist Church (opposite below)
The Baptists, or Anabaptists as they were still known in the early 19th century, were very well-established in Norwich and had several chapels. This one replaced a very commodious building which had already been greatly enlarged but "being too small for the congregation, who are numerous and very respectable" it was demolished. Its replacement built in 1811 at a cost of £5000, was "fronted with a grand colonnade of pillars, of the Doric order, approached by several steps, and inclosed with an iron railing". Blitzed during the war, a new Baptist chapel now stands on the site.

J.S. 1828.

ST PETERS WESLEYAN CHAPEL

Princes Street Congregational Church (opposite above)
When 20 year old John Alexander completed his month's unsuccessful trial as a new preacher at the Countess of Huntingdon's Tabernacle and was not to be offered the post that he had come to Norwich hoping to obtain, he preached on the text "Weeping may endure for a night, but joy cometh in the morning". He later said that this was "the text that founded Princes Street". 400 people asked him to stay and within two years he and his break-away congregation laid the foundation stone for a new chapel in Princes St. It was rebuilt and enlarged in 1869.

St Peters Chapel, Lady Lane (opposite below)
The Methodists were relative newcomers to the world of Norwich nonconformity and in 1753 St Marys Baptist church had said that "It is unlawful for any to attend upon the meeting of the Methodists". The chapel shown here, was built in 1824 to take the overflow from their Calvert Street Chapel that had been built in 1810, but soon St Peters became so fashionable that Calvert Street's pew rents fell from £228 to £81.This chapel, like Lady Lane itself, disappeared to make way for the Central Library in the early 1960s but the congregation had already moved to Park Lane.

Willow Lane Roman Catholic Chapel (below)
While the Duke of Norfolk still had a palace here, Catholics could use his private chapel but he stormed out of Norwich in 1711 and it wasn't until 1794 that a new catholic chapel (now the Maddermarket Theatre) was built in the garden of Strangers Hall. There was also a small chapel in St Swithins lane "the inside of which is adorned in the manner of the church of Rome" but in 1828, just as the Catholic Emancipation Act was passing, John Patience designed this stylish church for the Jesuits. Later used as a school, it ceased to have any religious connection many years ago.

The Gates and Walls

Norwich is like a great volume with a bad cover, having at best but parchment walls about it. Nor can it with much cost and time be effectually fortified because under the frowning brow of Moushold-hill, hanging over it, the river Yare, so wanton, that it knoweth not its own mind which way to go, such the involved flexures thereof within a mile of this city, runneth partly by, partly through it, but contributeth very little to the strengthning thereof.
Thomas Fuller 1662

You proceed to the Citty which is walled round full of towers, except on the river side which serves for the wall; they seeme the best in repaire of any walled citty I know, tho' in some places there are little breaches, but the carving and battlements and towers look well;
Celia Fiennes 1698

The walls of this city are reckoned three miles in circumference, taking in more ground than the city of London; but much of that ground lying open in pasture-fields and gardens; nor does it seem to be, like some ancient places, a decayed declining town, and that the walls mark out its ancient dimensions; but the walls seem to be placed, as if they expected that the city would in time increase sufficently to fill them up with buildings
Daniel Defoe 1722

If the City Gates were totally erased, the air and prospect to and from the town, would be much improved. When cities were surrounded by walls and gates, the state of the times made precautions necessary; but now that the system of war, and the police of the country is better understood and practiced, they become a nuisance, that smells rank in the nose of modern improvement! At least,if taking down the Gates be not thought necessary, the Walls, it is hoped, will be levelled.
The Norwich Directory or Gentlemen and Tradesmens Assistant March 1783

Norwich was enclosed by a wide defensive ditch in 1252 and in 1294 the City Wall was begun. Although they were said to be completed in 1320, it is Richard Spynk who has always been credited with finishing the job and supplying the gates and towers with "warlike instruments" in 1341 for which great service a grateful City quitted him and his descendants of taxes and tolls "for ever". By 1809 the last city gate was demolished although their names lived on, until recently , in the cries of bus conductors calling out the stops. (All these illustrations of the Gates were drawn by John Ninham between 1792 and '93 and all the quotations are from Browne's 1814 History.)

King Street Gates or South Gates, (opposite above)
"A small mean building, taken down in 1793. The city wall, from the gate to the river is in ruins."

Ber Street Gates, (above)
"One of the first to be erected. In the year 1726 it was taken down, and rebuilt with red brick in a very neat manner. Over the arch, in the inside, the city arms were placed, the south side was entirely removed, and that on the north converted into a residence for the keeper . . . The arch was pulled down in 1807, and not long after the tower was demolished, and the way laid open.

In the city wall, on the south side of the church (St Johns), were two towers. One of them, called the Watch Tower, was loftier than any of the others, and used anciently to exhibit lights. It had been for many years in a state of decay, when on Sunday, January 18, 1807, about noon,it fell down, and also a great part of the wall, with a tremendous crash, beating down with it all the outhouses adjoining, by which four cows were killed, but fortunately no person received any injury."

Brazen Doors or New Gates (above)
"The last to be erected of any of the city gates, the distance between Ber-street and St Stephen's gates being found too long; this afterwards obtained the name of Brazen-doors". In 1770 part of the adjoining wall on the east of the gate, fell down demolishing two newly-built houses but luckily nobody was injured. Note the two buildings by Thomas Ivory; the one on the left built in 1778 and on the right 1771, both still stand but the gate was demolished in 1793. These gates had been re-inforced with iron in the past – hence the name "Brazen".

St Stephens Gates (opposite)
Because of its situation, this was the principal City Gate and the one from which Elizabeth I entered, as did Will Kemp on his "Nine dayes wonder" in 1599 but which had defied the Earl of Warwick 50 years earlier. Browne called it "a large building, in the most gloomy style of ancient fortification; it consisted of a gothic arch of stone; over it was a chamber, which had formerly been an hermitage, and afterwards a chapel". The Gate was in good repair until 1793 when, with several others, it was demolished.

BALDWIN & ST

St Giles Gates (opposite)
Falling into decay, this gate was taken down in 1792. This was the road to Cambridge, Ely, Huntingdon, Peterborough and the North.

St Benedicts Gates or Westwick Gates (above)
Another casualty of 1793 when John De Carle and Philip Barnes demolished five gates for £60 as part of a contract of the previous year. Close by stood Heigham Gates, also known as Hell Gate; "it was an ancient mean building, and never a passage of much traffic, being originally only a postern". It fell down sometime at the beginning of the Eighteenth Century and was never rebuilt and was therefore not available for John Ninham to draw. The term Hell Gate, for Heigham, was said to be used in contrast to St Benedicts being known as Heaven Gate because it was the route pilgrims took on their way to Walsingham. It could, more likely, be that the term Hellgate was used in the Anglo-Danish sense to denote the lowness of the street hereabouts.

St Martins Gates or Coslany Gates (above)
"It was taken down in 1808, and the passage laid open. The west side of it adjoins a small piece of wall at the end of which is the remains of a tower with several arches, but it is going very fast to ruin". Such was the case in 1814. For a short distance, from Westwick street, the river Wensum served the purpose of a wall until it neared this gate where a stretch of wall ran down to the river.

St Augustines Gates (opposite)
This was demolished in 1794. "The city wall from this gate to Magdalen gate is partly built upon within side, and the towers converted into cottages; on the outside it is nearly built up, with some of the best buildings which are to be found on the walls."

The
Wheel

Magdalen Gates (above)
Anciently called Fye-bridge Gate, this was demolished in 1808 and was said to be the last to go. In 1814, several towers and about 300 yards of wall "now lie buried in their own ruins, having fallen down through decay and neglect".

Pockthorpe Gates or Bar Gates (opposite)
The name means Little Thorpe to distinguish this hamlet, which lay just outside the gates, from the adjoining parish.The area had a dubious legal status, even in the early 19th century, because the dean and chapter owned the manor and still held their courts there whilst the city claimed full jurisdiction over it. As to the Gates,they were taken down in 1792.

"A little to the north, at the turn of the wall, is a large tower, now converted into a dwelling-house, and the wall between it and the site of the gate is built up on the outside; from the gate the wall extends to the river side, where it finishes with a round tower, now converted into a cottage; and there are a few more built on the inside of the wall". From here, all the way to the boom Towers at Carrow, the river served in place of a wall.

Bishops Gates (below)
Not to be confused with Bishopgate (where gate means way) this structure was built and maintained by the Bishops of Norwich till 1393 when the city took over ownership and made it part of the defences.

"The gate was a neat gothic building (by far the lightest and handsomest of any of the city gates) the upper part was crowned with a battlement, and at the extremities were four turrets." It was the first of the city gates to be demolished in 1791.

Public Buildings and Streets

We took a walk over the City in the morning, and we both agreed that it was the finest City in England by far, in the center of it is a high Hill and on that a prodigious large old Castle almost perfect and forms a compleat square, round it is a fine Terrass Walk which commands the whole City. There are 36 noble Churches mostly built with Flint, besides many meeting Houses of divers sorts. A noble River runs almost thro the Center of the City. The City walls are also very perfect and all round the City but where the River is.
Parson Woodforde April 14 1775

The City of Norwich is one of the most considerable in England after London; it stands on more ground than any other but in numbers of inhabitants, some assert an equality. Arthur Young 1771

It is an immensely large place, but the streets in general are very ugly, and they are so ill-paved and dirty, as almost entirely to take away the pleasure of Walking. Dorothy Wordsworth 1778

It *was even in Camden's time reckoned among the most considerable cities in Britain, for the industry of its citizens, their loyalty to their prince, and civility to foreigners; as well as for wealth, number of people, and neatness of their buildings.* Chase's Directory 1783

For Society, of all the places I have ever seen, Norwich is the best. Robert Southey 1801

St Andrews Hall (above) from a print of 1851

The Guildhall (above)
Built between the years 1407 and 1453, this was the seat of civic government in Norwich until 1938, when the City Hall was opened. In 1511 the roof fell in and in 1635 the hall became unsafe when saltpetre diggers mined three feet below the foundations and "would not forbear till some of the aldermen attended the kings council at London and obtained an order for them to desist". In the cells below, Thomas Bilney (the most famous of the Norwich martyrs) was held, before being burnt.

Outside the Guildhall, the Market Place looked, in this print by David Hodgson, much as it had done over a century earlier when Celia Fiennes described "stalls for the Country butchers . . . on the other side are houses of the Town butchers. By it is a large market for fish which are all a little distance from the heart of the City so it is not annoy'd with them, there is also a very large Market place and Hall and Cross for fruite and little things every day, and also a place under pillars for the Corn Market."

Chases Directory of 1783 said "In the Market-Place, the Lower or Gentleman's Walk should be flagged and posted off from the carriageway, for a parade, exchange, or place of business and pleasure. This, tho' it might cost something considerable, would very much enhance the value of the shops and dwellings on the walk, and afford gentlemen and merchants an opportunity of meeting to transact business, or to amuse themselves in walking and conversation".

Market Place, looking south-west, (opposite above)
This print, from the Beauties of England and Wales of 1812, shows the other end of the market to the above print and is from the same period. Note the stall-holders shelters.

The Fish Market. (opposite below)
This print, by the same artist as that of the Guildhall, shows the area now occupied by the War Memorial.

COLDHAM
POPES. HEAD. INN
PORTER. ALE

HOWARD
LATE LOWDEN

Two views of the Market looking north (opposite top) **and south** (opposite bottom).
The existence of the staue of Wellington, dates this print to 1854 or shortly thereafter.

The Assembly House (below)
The College of St Mary in the Fields, one of the largest religious foundations in Norwich, was begun in 1250 and, upon the dissolution, granted to Miles Spencer, its last dean. Henry Hobart, Earl of Buckinghamshire having inherited it, sold a part of the site to a consortium, of which he and architect Thomas Ivory were members and in 1754 Ivory began the present structure. "An elegant building of red brick, 200 feet, consisting of two handsome rooms, fitted up in a style of much elegance as well as convenience; the partition between them is so contrived that it may be occasionally removed, and the two rooms laid into one, thereby forming a ball-room exceeded by few in the kingdom. The cielings are of very neat stucco work, from which are suspended several chandeliars of cut glass, with corresponding lustres on the sides of the room. The other parts of the house are disposed into smaller rooms for card parties &c. In the front is a spacious vestibule,and on the back part of the building a recess, in which is a refectory, where wines, tea,coffee &c. are distributed to the company".

A ball to celebrate the Peace of Amiens in 1802 was described thus "The Mayor's ball was very splendid as to numbers, the dancing very crowded in the Tea Room and a cold supper with hot soups in the Great Room, three tables from top to botom and above 50 people not sitting. (The Mayor's wife) Mrs Ive's dame d'honneur sat by her at supper, on the other side Miss Drake and by her that Handsome Fair Quaker Gurney from Earlham".

After being a school and a shoe warehouse, the building was restored to its original use through the generosity of H.J.Sexton in 1951.

Theatre Royal (below)
Opened on 31 January 1758, with Congreve's *Way of the World*, this was the wonderful Thomas Ivory's third major building in three years after the Octagon Chapel and the Assembly House (and in this case, he was of the proprietor of the undertaking). Having set up the theatre Ivory sold over 90% of the business in 1768. In 1799 it came into the possession of another Norwich architect William Wilkins. He rebuilt it in 1800 because, as he had said the year before, "The Entrance & Avenues are so ill-conceived that only one person can approach the Lobby, a lady must be seperated from the arm of her protector both on entering & leaving the Lobby. The Audience from the Boxes, Green Boxes & Pit are huddled together & on leaving the House they must pass singly to the entrance where they are obliged to run the Gauntlet thro' Coachmen, Footmen & Porters & . . . it really is otherwise impossible that Ladies can reach their carriages without danger of spoiling their dresses and being squeezed perhaps between Doorkeepers, Porters, and prostitutes".

The theatre's patent permitted it to open only from 1st of January till the 1st of June and in assize week. For the rest of the year the patentee and performers toured on the following circuit: June, Yarmouth; July, Ipswich; August Yarmouth; September, Cambridge; October, Bury; November, Colchester; and December, Ipswich.

Many great stars appeared and there were outstanding successes such as Sara Siddons in 1788 in *The Bleeding Nun of Lindenburg*; and in 1815 *The Rebellion of Norwich in 1549* was staged, but in 1818, when Eliza O'Neill appeared in *Venice Preserved* "no law prevailed but that of the strongest. There were shrieks, reproaches, lamentations, bonnets were cramped up, hats squeezed flat, gowns torn". In the most Jacobin city in England, this republican play was a sell-out, "families of the highest respectability were in inconvenient situations. Even the orchestra pit was occupied by the public".

The Norfolk and Norwich Hospital (above)
Founded in 1771 by William Fellowes "this great ornament of the city was begun, completed and supported by voluntary contributions. The government of this hospital is vested in a committee of the subscribers, who meet every Saturday at eleven o'clock in the forenoon, to transact the necessary business: they have the appointment of a treasurer, three physicians, three surgeons, an assistant, a secretary, an apothecary, who resides in and rules the house, with the assitance of a matron".

In 1789 Parson Woodforde recalled one of the inspections by the committee who would ask the patients how they were being treated: "Before Tea I walked to the Norfolk and Norwich Hospital with Mr Priest who is one of the Visitors for this week and we walked over almost the whole Hospital into almost every Ward, and I think I never saw an Hospital kept in a better and more clean, airy manner. All the poor Creatures in it appeared quite cheerful and grateful in their present Complaints." Woodforde was one of many who attended the Musical Concerts during Assize week when on the Thursday there was "the anniversary sermon at the cathedral for the support of the Norfolk and Norwich Hospital – a grand performance of sacred music; there is a ball at the assembly-house, and the theatre is open; public breakfasting at the gardens in the morning with concerts and fireworks at night". In 1824 the first Triennial Music Festival was founded in aid of the hospital and held its concerts, as it still does, in St Andrews Hall.

Hochstetter's Map 1789 (overleaf)
By this time the population of the City was just over 40,000, although it would decline slightly during the Napoleonic Wars. Virtually all the citizens lived inside the Walls, the only exceptions being those in Pockthorpe Street and Heigham Street and the villages, like Eaton and Earlham, that lay within the Liberty. A Pleasure Garden and the new Norfolk and Norwich Hospital stood just outside St Stephen's Gates, but apart from a few merchants houses they were the only significant buildings outside the Walls.

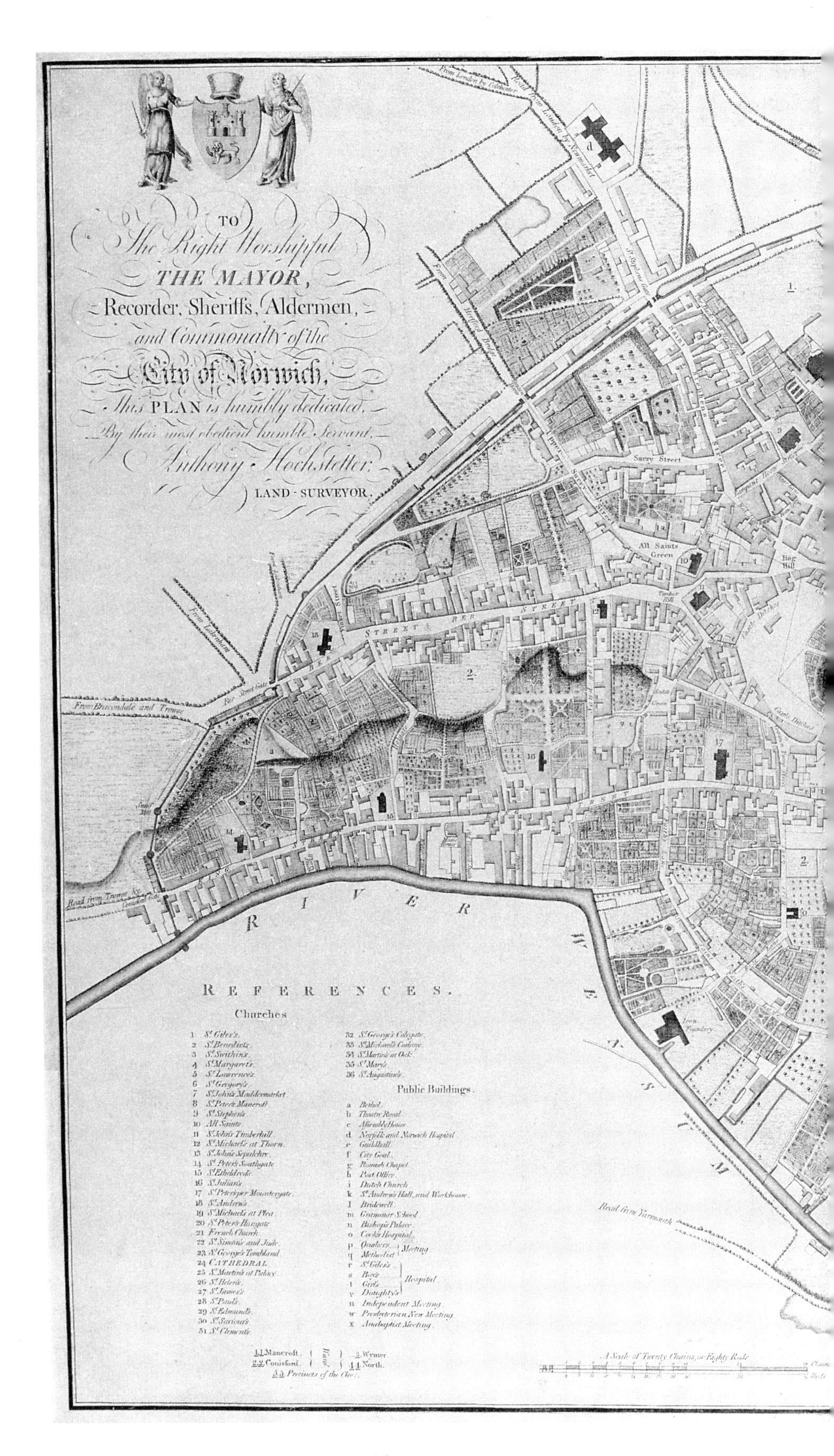
TO
The Right Worshipful
THE MAYOR,
Recorder, Sheriffs, Aldermen,
and Commonalty of the
City of Norwich,
This PLAN is humbly dedicated,
By their most obedient humble Servant,
Anthony Hochstetter
LAND-SURVEYOR.
Surry Street
All Saints Green
Ber Street
River
REFERENCES.
Churches
1 St. Giles's.
2 St. Benedicts.
3 St. Swithins.
4 St. Margaret's.
5 St. Lawrence's.
6 St. Gregory's.
7 St. John's Maddermarket.
8 St. Peter's Mancroft.
9 St. Stephens.
10 All Saints.
11 St. John's Timberhill.
12 St. Michael's at Thorn.
13 St. John's Sepulchre.
14 St. Peter's Southgate.
15 St. Etheldreds.
16 St. Julians.
17 St. Peter's per Mountergate.
18 St. Andrew's.
19 St. Michaels at Plea.
20 St. Peter's Hungate.
21 French Church.
22 St. Simon's and Jude.
23 St. George's Tombland.
24 CATHEDRAL.
25 St. Martin's at Palace.
26 St. Helen's.
27 St. James's.
28 St. Paul's.
29 St. Edmund's.
30 St. Saviour's.
31 St. Clements.
32 St. George's Colegate.
33 St. Michael's Coslany.
34 St. Martin's at Oak.
35 St. Mary's.
36 St. Augustine's.
Public Buildings.
a Bethel.
b Theatre Royal.
c Assembly House.
d Norfolk and Norwich Hospital.
e Guildhall.
f City Goal.
g Romish Chapel.
h Post Office.
i Dutch Church.
k St. Andrew's Hall, and Workhouse.
l Bridewell.
m Grammar School.
n Bishop's Palace.
o Cook's Hospital.
p Quakers Meeting
q Methodist Meeting
r St. Giles's Hospital
s Boys Hospital
t Girls Hospital
v Doughty's Hospital
u Independent Meeting.
w Presbyterian New Meeting.
x Anabaptist Meeting.
1.1. Mancroft.
2.2. Conisford.
3. Wymer.
4.4. North.
Ward
5.5. Precincts of the Clo.
A Scale of Twenty Chains, or Eighty Rods
Road from Yarmouth
Iron Foundery

PLAN
of
The CITY of NORWICH,
Deſcribing the Streets, Lanes,
Public Edifices & Buildings &c.
Divided
Into its reſpective WARDS
Survey'd by Anthony Hochstetter;
Engrav'd by Samuel John Neele,
No. 352, Strand,
LONDON.
1789
Saint Martins at Oak Street
Gilden Croft
To Catton

St Andrews Hall (above)
This was formerly the convent church of the Dominican, or Black, Friars.The present structure was that which was re-built by Sir Thomas Erpingham and, after his death in 1428, completed by his son Robert who was a friar of this convent. Originally dedicated to John the Baptist, it was designed on the scale of a cathedral, with the nave separated from the chancel by a six-sided tower (which fell down in 1712) . At the time of the Reformation, the leading citizens petitioned Henry VIII to grant this building to the City in whose possession it has remained ever since, fufilling a succession of functions. At various times, before and after the Reformation, the Corporation have used it for civic services in preference to the Cathedral.

In 1566 the chancel (called Blackfriars Hall) was given to the Dutch congregation as their church and there was still an annual service conducted here in Dutch until the First World War. In 1336 a colony of Dutch and Flemish weavers had been asked to settle in Norwich to give a much-needed boost to the weaving trade and in 1566 30 families, fleeing from Spanish persecution in the Netherlands, were invited (although about 170 were already here). Within 20 years there were 6000 and this was their church. (Those of "The Wallon Company" were given the church of St Mary in nearby Queen Street.)

Chases Directory of 1783 said "the ground that has been levelled and cleaned in front of St Andrews Hall, is one of the few improvements the city has lately received. Had the area been still more open and extended, the alteration had been more perfect."

The ShireHall (below)
This engraving by R Ransome was produced in 1824, when the ShireHall was newly built. The architect was William Wilkins who had won a competion to design it in 1821. It had been intended to stand on the top of the mound next to the Castle but that site was used for the prison building which he designed in 1825. His father was a famous local architect who had re-modelled the Castle interior in 1792-3, and restored the Erpingham Gate and the West Front of the Cathedral. Both men were proprietors of the Theatre Royal and both rebuilt it (1800 and 1826) but to make matters even more confusing the older man's father (also William) had also been one of the first of the theatre's joint-owners in 1768. The designer of the Shire Hall had already built Nelson's Column in Yarmouth and was to be architect of the National Gallery and the Frontage of Kings College Cambridge.

This building "Exhibits the Tudor style of architecture, and is a substantial edifice of brick, cement in imitation of stone, and possessing all the usual accommodations. Attatched to the crown court is a small room called the prisoners lobby, communicating with the cells on castle hill, from whence prisoners are brought by a descending shaft, through a substantial passage". It is now part of the Castle Museum.

THE
BLACK
CHEQUERS
FINCH'S

ON CHARING CROSS, NORWICH.

Four Street Scenes: (opposite)
House in Elm Hill, (top left) **Cowgate**, (top right) **Sir Thomas Erpingham's Window**, (bottom left) **Entrance to Strangers Hall** (bottom right)
These views of Norwich are all by Henry Ninham. The house in Elm Hill is No 18 and was the home of Elisha DeHague, Town Clerk and a prominent figure in literary and social circles at the start of the 19th century. The house, only slightly altered, is now a shop; in the view of Cowgate, only the Cathedral remains while Sir Thomas Erpingham's window that once stood round the left corner of the Cowgate view and was saved when its house was demolished for the Victorian Gas Works, now stands round the other corner in a house at Palace Plain next door to John Cotman's old home. As for Strangers Hall, the Lion and Unicorn Canopy over the street entrance was removed after the War.

Cow Tower (below)
This ancient tower, the oldest brick structure in Norwich, was built originally as a prison for the Cathedral although the Prior also used it at one time to collect river tolls. It was transferred to the City in 1378 some years after it had been given, with its adjoining land, to the Great Hospital who had allowed it get into a ruinous condition. It was repaired or rebuilt in 1390 and "in 1565 it was hired by Lord Maltravers, (for what purpose is not known). Since that time no use has been made of it, and it is going fast to decay." So said Browne in 1814.

Today it is safe and bears the scars of the damage it sustained during Ketts Rebellion, when Miles the Gunner, firing from the Rebels' Camp on Mousehold, perforated its battlements.

Doorway, The Old Barge, King Street (opposite)

When, in1817, John Cotman etched this medieval doorway, recycled from the nearby Austin friary, the view across the river from the yard of the Old Barge would have been of relatively inaccessible pasture-land and gentle hills. Chase's Directory of 1783 had complained "At no place is a bridge more wanted than at King Street Gate; by which the time and trouble of going round by Bishopgate Bridge would be saved by many". Then in 1810, both Carrow Bridge and Foundry Bridge were built, both with new connections to the Yarmouth Road and within 30 years the view across the river from the inn yard would be one of railway yards.

Thorpe Station and Foundry Bridge (below)

Despite such brave schemes as "Norwich a Port", the City had suffered a serious decline in trade as readier access to cheaper transport and materials gave other centres an advantage. An over-dependence on the cloth trade and a reliance on traditional skills at a time of mass-mechanisation, had been a serious problem for Norwich in the 1820s. Edward Taylor, music critic of the Spectator, said of it in 1833 "placed in a corner of the kingdom, dirty, crooked, old-fashioned Norwich is never heard of or known to exist except when dragged into infamous notoriety by its corrupt electors, or held up to more honourable notice for its unrivalled triennial festival". Such a statement would have been unthinkable less than 20 years earlier. Since Elizabeth I's reign Norwich had been the second City in size, wealth and population. Suddenly things had changed.

The first railway to be built in Norwich was that to Yarmouth in 1844. It was designed by the great George Stephenson and soon there were two companies with lines to London, Victoria Station being built on the site of the former Pleasure Gardens at St Stephens Gates. Harriet Martineau soon complained: "railways, free trade, and cheap publications have much to do with the extinction of the celebrity of ancient Norwich, in regard both to its material and intellectual productions. Its bombazine manufacture has gone to Yorkshire, and its literary fame to the four winds". She was wrong, at least as far as railways were concerned. Soon Norwich would revive and diversify and the railway would play a big part in giving the City new prospects and opportunities. But that is part of another story.

Index

Picture Credits: The pictures marked with an asterisk* were kindly supplied from the Ron Fiske Collection. The three maps on pages 4, 24, & 56 were kindly supplied by Mr Raymond Frostick and appear in his excellent book *The Printed Plans of Norwich.*

Printed in Great Britain by St Edmundsbury Press Ltd,
Bury St Edmunds, Suffolk